Health and Safety
Commission

Health and Safety (Firs

Approved Code of Practice and Gui...

London: HMSO

© *Crown copyright 1990*
First published 1990
Revised 1991

General enquiries regarding this publication should be addressed to the Health and Safety Executive at one of the following public enquiry points:

Library and Information Services
Broad Lane
SHEFFIELD S3 7HQ
Telephone: (0742) 752539 Telex: 54556

Library and Information Services
Baynards House
1 Chepstow Place
Westbourne Grove
LONDON W2 4TF
Telephone: 071-221 0870 Telex: 25683

ISBN 0 11 885536 0

Notice of Approval *v*

Preface *vi*

Introduction *1*

Regulation 1 Citation and commencement *2*

Regulation 2 Interpretation *2*

Regulation 3 Duty of employer to make provision for first-aid *2*

Different work activities need different provisions *2*
The situation when access to treatment is difficult *2*
Employees working away from employer's premises *3*
Employees of more than one employer working together *3*
First-aid provision for persons other than an employer's own employees and for trainees *3*
Deciding on first-aid equipment and facilities *4*
First-aid boxes and kits *4*
Travelling first-aid kits *5*
Supplementary equipment *5*
First-aid room and equipment *6*
Suitable persons *8*
Criteria for deciding adequate and appropriate provision of first-aiders *8*
Provision of first-aiders when access to treatment is difficult *9*
Provision of first-aiders when employees of more than one employer are working together *9*
Provision of first-aiders when employees work away from employer's premises *9*
Number of employees and appointed persons *9*
Recruitment and selection of first-aiders *9*
Appropriate training for first-aiders *10*
Access to skilled advice *10*
Recording first-aid treatment *10*
Approval of first-aid training and qualifications *10*
Refresher courses *12*
First-aid training where specific hazards exist *12*
Emergency first-aid training *13*
First-aid trainers and examiners *13*
First-aid examinations *14*
Training for first-aid lay trainers *14*

Regulation 4 Duty of employer to inform his employees of the arrangements made in connection with first-aid *15*

Regulation 5 Duty of self-employed person to provide first-aid equipment *16*

Regulation 6 Power to grant exemptions *16*

Regulation 7 Cases where these Regulations do not apply *17*

Regulation 8 Application to miscellaneous mines *17*

Regulation 9 Application offshore *17*

Regulation 10 Repeals, revocations and modification *18*

Schedule 1	Repeals *19*	
Schedule 2	Revocations *19*	
Appendix 1	Addresses of Employment Nursing Advisers *22*	
Appendix 2	Format for recording first-aid treatment *25*	
Annexe	General first-aid guidance for inclusion in first-aid boxes *26*	

Notice of Approval

By virtue of section 16(4) of the Health and Safety at Work etc Act 1974 and with the consent of the Secretary of State for Employment the Health and Safety Commission has on 12 February 1990 approved the revised Code of Practice entitled *First Aid at Work*.

The revised Approved Code of Practice gives practical guidance with respect to the Health and Safety (First-Aid) Regulations 1981 (SI 1981 No 917) and replaces the original Approved Code of Practice which was issued in 1982.

The revised Approved Code of Practice comes into effect on 2 July 1990.

Signed

M F DOWNING
Secretary to the Health and Safety Commission

12 February 1990

Preface

1   The Health and Safety (First-Aid) Regulations 1981, SI 1981 No. 917, which were made on 29 June 1981 and came into operation on 1 July 1982, place a general duty on employers to make, or ensure that there is made, adequate first-aid provision for their employees if they are injured or become ill at work. Employers must also inform their employees of the first-aid provision made for them. Self-employed persons are also required by the regulations to provide adequate and appropriate equipment, so that first aid can be rendered if they are injured or become ill at work.

2   The Approved Code of Practice for the Health and Safety (First-Aid) Regulations 1981, approved by the Health and Safety Commission, with the consent of the Secretary of State for Employment, gives practical guidance for employers and self-employed persons on how they may meet the requirements of the Regulations.

3   The guidance notes published by the Health and Safety Executive supplement the Regulations and Approved Code and give advice on such matters as equipment and training. In this publication all quotations from the Regulations will be printed in italics.

4   Throughout this document, paragraphs are marked to indicate whether they are Regulations, Approved Code of Practice (ACOP) or Guidance Notes (Guidance). In addition the paragraphs are colour coded as follows:

   Regulations

   ACOP

   Guidance

Where there is either no ACOP to accompany the Regulations, or Guidance notes to accompany the ACOP, it can be taken that the Regulations or ACOP stand alone.

5   The treatment of minor illnesses such as the administration of tablets and/or medicines falls outside the definition of first aid in the Health and Safety (First-Aid) Regulations 1981. For this reason, the treatment of minor illnesses does not form part of the training of a first-aider. Therefore no references to equipment or facilities for the treatment of minor illnesses are included in the guidance notes.

6   Where a full-time occupational health service which is in the charge of a registered medical practitioner or qualified occupational health nurse is provided by an employer, the first-aid arrangements for the establishment should be made by the registered medical practitioner or qualified occupational health nurse in charge. These arrangements may differ from those set out in the Approved Code provided that they are of at least equivalent standard. The occupational health service need not be staffed continuously by a full-time registered medical practitioner or qualified occupational health nurse, provided that arrangements are made by him/her for suitable coverage for all employees during working hours. Where first-aid arrangements are not made by the registered medical practitioner or qualified occupational health nurse, the arrangements should comply with the Approved Code of Practice.

7   Changes in the Approved Code of Practice (1990)

The main changes are:

(a)   employers assessing the need for first aid in their workplace should apply less emphasis on 'numbers of employees' as a criterion for deciding what first-aid provision is adequate and appropriate. Experience has shown that the number of employees is often the only factor considered in deciding what provision should be made. This approach detracts from the main philosophy of flexibility contained in the regulations as well as ignoring the significance of other criteria which may be more important;

(b) 'occupational first-aiders' are no longer regarded as 'suitable persons' who will count as first-aiders under the regulations. Comparatively few people have been trained as occupational first-aiders since the regulations came into force, and employers' obligations under the regulations are better met by arranging for first-aiders to be trained in specific techniques appropriate to the circumstances of the undertaking;

(c) where special first-aid techniques require specified items of equipment, these should be available in addition to the standard first-aid equipment; and

(d) foreseeable absences of first-aiders, such as planned annual leave, are not considered 'exceptional and temporary circumstances' during which the substitution for a first-aider by an appointed person is justified.

8   Changes in the guidance notes (1990):

(a) the list of items for first-aid boxes and kits has been modified;

(b) guidance on the recruitment and selection of first-aiders has been expanded;

(c) 'occupational first-aiders' are no longer referred to in the guidance notes;

(d) guidance on specific training for first-aiders is included in the guidance notes;

(e) alterations have been made to the criteria for approving the training and qualifications of first-aiders and lay trainers;

(f) there is no longer separate guidance for small employers;

(g) the minimum length of the refresher course for first-aiders has been increased from one day to two.

1   The Code of Practice set out in this booklet has been approved by the Health and Safety Commission with the consent of the Secretary of State under section 16 of the Health and Safety at Work etc Act 1974. It gives practical guidance on the requirements placed on employers and self-employed persons by the Health and Safety (First-Aid) Regulations 1981 and takes effect on 2 July 1990.

Although failure to observe any provision of this Code is not in itself an offence, that failure may be taken by a court in criminal proceedings as proof that a person has contravened a regulation to which the provision relates. In such a case, however, it will be open to that person to satisfy the court that the regulation has been complied with in some other way.

2   The Regulations and Approved Code of Practice are intended to provide a framework within which every undertaking can develop effective first-aid arrangements. The guidance notes are intended to supplement the framework of the Regulations and Approved Code of Practice. They include advice on requirements to be followed and action to be taken by employers in order to comply with the law, but they are essentially notes of guidance. The Health and Safety Executive (HSE) will from time to time further review the advice given here in the light of developments in first-aid knowledge and will issue up-to-date advice in revised guidance.

3   In this Approved Code of Practice, unless the context requires otherwise:

(a)   'employer' includes the manager of any mine to which the Regulations apply (see Regulation 7(e) and 8 of the Regulations);

(b)   'first aid' has the same meaning as in Regulation 2 of the Regulations;

(c)   'registered medical practitioner' means a medical practitioner registered under the Medical Act 1983;

(d)   'qualified occupational health nurse' means a nurse whose name is entered in Part 1 of the single professional register maintained by the United Kingdom Central Council for Nursing, Midwifery and Health Visiting, and who holds the Occupational Health Nursing Certificate of the Royal College of Nursing; or the Birmingham Accident Hospital Certificate gained between 1941 and 1973; or other equivalent certificate of training in occupational health nursing;

(e)   'the Regulations' means the Health and Safety (First-Aid) Regulations 1981; and other words and expressions used which are also used in the Health and Safety at Work etc Act 1974 have the same meaning as in that Act.

Regulation 1

Citation and commencement

These Regulations may be cited as the Health and Safety (First-Aid) Regulations 1981 and shall come into operation on 1st July 1982.

Regulation 2

Interpretation

(1) In these Regulations, unless the context otherwise requires - "first-aid" means -

(a) in cases where a person will need help from a medical practitioner or nurse, treatment for the purpose of preserving life and minimising the consequences of injury and illness until such help is obtained, and

(b) treatment of minor injuries which would otherwise receive no treatment or which do not need treatment by a medical practitioner or nurse;

"mine" means a mine within the meaning of section 180 of the Mines and Quarries Act 1954[a]

(2) In these Regulations, unless the context otherwise requires, any reference to -

(a) a numbered Regulation or Schedule is a reference to the Regulation of, or Schedule to, these Regulations bearing that number;

(b) a numbered paragraph is a reference to the paragraph bearing that number in the Regulation in which the reference appears.

(a) 1954 c. 70; relevant amending instrument is S.I. 1974/2013.

Regulation 3

Duty of employer to make provision for first-aid

(1) An employer shall provide, or ensure that there are provided, such equipment and facilities as are adequate and appropriate in the circumstances for enabling first-aid to be rendered to his employees if they are injured or become ill at work.

Different work activities need different provisions

1 Different work activities involve different hazards and therefore different first-aid provision is required. Some establishments (eg offices or libraries) have relatively low hazards whereas others (eg factories and chemical works) often have a greater degree of hazard or specific hazard. Requirements for first-aid provision at work will therefore largely depend on the type of work being carried out.

The situation when access to treatment is difficult

2 When access to places of treatment outside the establishment is difficult, consideration should be given as to whether a first-aid room should be provided. In addition, the local ambulance service should be informed of the location of the establishment and the nature of the work being undertaken. This is particularly important when the work is potentially hazardous.

Employees working away from employer's premises

3   Where employees are sent to work away from their employer's establishment, their employer will still have to ensure adequate and appropriate first-aid provision is made for them. The requirements will vary according to the nature of the work activity and its associated risks, and whether the employees work alone or in small or large groups.

4   In the case of peripatetic employees in urban areas working where there are relatively low hazards, eg sales, delivery of non-hazardous substances, inspection or other similar work, an employer may not need to make available full first-aid facilities for these employees other than the permanent provision at their establishment.

5   In the case of employees who regularly work away from their employer's establishment in isolated locations or where they are involved in travelling long distances in remote areas from which access to accident and emergency facilities may be difficult, it may be necessary for first-aid equipment to be carried by, or made available to, employees where potentially dangerous tools or machinery are used. The equipment should be suitable for the numbers involved and the potential hazards to which the employees may be exposed.

Employees of more than one employer working together

6   Where employees of more than one employer are working together, and the employers concerned wish to avoid duplication of provision, they should make an agreement whereby one of them provides the necessary first-aid equipment and facilities; eg on construction sites, the contractors involved might agree that all the necessary first-aid provision will be made by the contractor who has the largest number of employees on site. The agreement should be in writing and a copy kept by each employer concerned. Where such an agreement is made, each employer should inform his own employees of the arrangements for first aid.

First-aid provision for persons other than an employer's own employees and for trainees

7   The regulations place requirements on employers only in respect of their own employees while they are at work. When making provision, there is no obligation on employers, under the regulations or ACOP, to take account of persons who are not their employees, eg pupils in schools, visitors to cinemas or theatres, customers in shops etc. Employers whose premises are regularly attended by such persons may, however, wish to make some provision for them.

8   Where first-aid facilities are provided for both employees and visitors, care should be taken that the level of first-aid provision available to employees is not allowed to fall below the standard set out in the Approved Code of Practice. First-aid provision for persons not at work in some cases is governed by other legislation or by official guidance (eg first-aid provision on public service vehicles is covered by Regulations made under the Road Traffic Act 1960; the Department of Education and Science issues guidance on first-aid provision for pupils in schools). It should be noted that the Approved Code of Practice and the guidance notes do not replace or lessen the force of such provisions. Trainees covered by the Health and Safety (Training for Employment) Regulations 1988, have the same status as employees under health and safety legislation. The person immediately providing training to such a trainee is regarded as the employer of that trainee.

Deciding on first-aid equipment and facilities

9   The criteria for deciding the scale and type of first-aid equipment and facilities needed are those set out in 3(1) paragraphs 1-5. In all establishments first-aid provision should be readily available to each employee at all times. The equipment and facilities to be provided will vary according to the circumstances from a small travelling first-aid kit to a first-aid room. All establishments will need at least one first-aid box. Each box should be placed in a clearly identified and readily accessible location. Every first-aider should have access to first-aid equipment and, where appropriate, facilities.

10   In compact establishments, where a number of employees work in close proximity, first-aid equipment should be sited at a point convenient to the majority of the workforce or where there is greatest risk of an injury occurring. Where establishments have a large number of employees but are divided into a number of self-contained working areas, consideration should be given to setting up a main facility with supplementary equipment in each of these working areas. A large plant with a small number of employees dispersed over a wide area may require provision in different parts of the establishment.

11   Soap and water and disposable drying materials should be provided for first-aid purposes. Where soap and water are not available, individually wrapped moist cleansing wipes which are not impregnated with alcohol may be used. **The use of antiseptics is not necessary for the first-aid treatment of wounds.**

First-aid boxes and kits

12   First-aid boxes and travelling first-aid kits should contain a sufficient quantity of suitable first-aid materials **and nothing else**.

13   Contents of the boxes and kits should be replenished as soon as possible after use in order to ensure that there is always an adequate supply of all materials. Items should not be used after the expiry date shown on packets. It is therefore essential that first-aid equipment be checked frequently, to make sure there are sufficient quantities and all items are usable. Employers should note paragraph 5 of the preface in relation to treatment of minor illnesses.

14   First-aid boxes should be made of suitable material designed to protect the contents from damp and dust and should be clearly identified as first-aid containers: the marking used should be a white cross on a green background in accordance with the Safety Signs Regulations 1980.

15   First-aid boxes which are to form part of an establishment's permanent first-aid provision should contain only those items which a first-aider has been trained to use.

16   Sufficient quantities of each item should always be available in every first-aid box or container. In most cases these will be:

(a)   one guidance card (see Annexe);

(b)   twenty individually wrapped sterile adhesive dressings (assorted sizes) appropriate to the work environment (which may be detectable for the catering industry);

(c)   two sterile eye pads, with attachment;

(d)   six individually wrapped triangular bandages;

(e) six safety pins;

(f) six medium sized individually wrapped sterile unmedicated wound dressings (approx 10 cm x 8 cm);

(g) two large sterile individually wrapped unmedicated wound dressings (approx 13cm x 9cm); and

(h) three extra large sterile individually wrapped unmedicated wound dressings (approx 28cm x 17.5 cm).

Where mains tap water is not readily available for eye irrigation, sterile water or sterile normal saline (0.9%) in sealed disposable containers should be provided. Each container should hold at least 300 ml and should not be re-used once the sterile seal is broken. At least 900 ml should be provided. **Eye baths/eye cups/refillable containers should not be used for eye irrigation**.

17 Sterile first-aid dressings should be packaged in such a way as to allow the user to apply the dressing to a wound without touching that part which is to come into direct contact with the wound.

18 That part of the dressing which comes into contact with a wound should be absorbent. There should be a bandage or other fixture attached to the dressings and consequently there is no reason to keep scissors in the first-aid box. Dressings, including adhesive ones, should be of a design and type which is appropriate for their use.

19 Where an employee has received additional training in the treatment of specific hazards which require the use of special antidotes or special equipment, these may be stored near the hazard area or may be kept in the first-aid box.

Travelling first-aid kits

20 The contents of travelling first-aid kits should be appropriate for the circumstances in which they are to be used. At least the following should be included:-

(a) card giving the general first-aid guidance set out in the Annexe;

(b) six individually wrapped sterile adhesive dressings;

(c) one large sterile unmedicated dressing;

(d) two triangular bandages;

(e) two safety pins;

(f) individually wrapped moist cleansing wipes.

Supplementary equipment

21 Where an establishment covers a large area or is divided into a number of separate and self-contained working areas, it may be necessary to provide suitable (carrying) equipment for the transportation of casualties.

22 It is recommended that where blankets are provided, they should be stored alongside the equipment and in such a way as to keep them free from dust and damp.

23 Disposable plastic gloves and aprons and suitable protective equipment should be provided near the first-aid materials and should be properly stored

Guidance

and checked regularly to ensure that they remain in good condition.

24   Blunt-ended stainless steel scissors (minimum length 12.70 cm) should be kept where there is a possibility that clothing might have to be cut away. These should be kept along with items of protective clothing and equipment.

25   Plastic disposable bags for soiled or used first-aid dressings should be provided. Employers should ensure that used dressings etc are safely disposed of in sealed bags. Local authorities should be contacted for guidance on disposal.

ACOP

First-aid room and equipment

26   An employer whose establishment presents a high risk from hazards should provide a suitably equipped and staffed first-aid room. This provision should be considered in undertakings such as shipbuilding, chemical industries and large construction sites. When the location of the workplace makes access to accident and emergency facilities difficult or where there is dispersed working, the employer should decide whether a first-aid room may be needed. The need for a first-aid room is not solely dependent on the number of persons employed in the undertaking.

27   Where a first-aid room is appropriate for an establishment, the following conditions should be met:

(a)   A *'suitable person'* (3(2) paragraph 1) should be responsible for the room and its contents;

(b)   A *'suitable person'* (3(2) paragraph 1) should be available at all times when employees are at work;

(c)   The room should be readily available at all times when employees are at work and should not be used for any purposes other than the rendering of first-aid or health screening;

(d)   The room should be positioned as near as possible to a point of access for transport to hospital, taking into account the location and layout of the establishment;

(e)   The room should be large enough to hold a couch, with space for people to work around it, and a chair;

(f)   The room's entrances should be wide enough to accommodate a stretcher, wheelchair or carrying chair;

(g)   The room should contain suitable facilities and equipment, have an impervious floor covering and should be effectively ventilated, heated, lighted and maintained. All surfaces should be easy to clean. The room should be cleaned each working day and suitable arrangements for refuse disposal should be provided;

(h)   Suitable facilities (for example one or more chairs) should be provided close to the first-aid room if employees have to wait for treatment. These should be kept clean and maintained;

(i)   The room should be clearly identified as a first-aid room. Identification should be by means of a sign complying with the Safety Signs Regulations 1980; and

ACOP

(j) A notice should be attached to the door of the first-aid room clearly showing names and locations of the nearest first-aiders/appointed persons.

28 It is essential that in the event of an accident or sudden illness, immediate contact can be made with the 'suitable person' on call. Effective means of communication should therefore be provided between all work areas, the first-aid room and the first-aider on call. In most establishments the appropriate means will be a telephone link, but where the nature of the work undertaken, or the layout of an establishment, for example a construction site, is such that a telephone is not readily available in each work area, then other means of communication will be necessary.

3(1)

Guidance

29 When siting a new first-aid room the necessity to have toilets nearby and for the room to be on the ground floor should be considered. Corridors, lifts and doors etc, which lead to the first-aid room should allow access for a stretcher, wheelchair or carrying chair. Consideration should also be given to the possibility of providing some form of emergency lighting.

30 The following facilities and equipment should be provided in first-aid rooms:

(a) sink with running hot and cold water always available;

(b) drinking water when not available on tap and disposable cups;

(c) soap;

(d) paper towels;

(e) smooth topped working surfaces;

(f) a suitable store for first-aid materials;

(g) first-aid equipment equivalent in range and standard and quantities to those listed in 3(1) paragraph 16;

(h) suitable refuse containers lined with a disposable plastic bag (see 3(1) paragraph 25);

(i) a couch (with a waterproof surface) and frequently cleaned pillow and blankets;

(j) clean protective garments for use by first-aiders;

(k) a chair;

(l) an appropriate record book (see 3(2) paragraph 18); and

(m) a bowl.

Where special first-aid equipment is needed, this equipment may also be stored in the first-aid room.

31 First-aiders or appointed persons should be nominated by the management to see that the first-aid room is kept stocked to the required standard and that it is at all times clean and ready for immediate use.

3(1)

Regulation

(2) Subject to paragraphs (3) and (4), an employer shall provide, or ensure that there is provided, such number of suitable persons as is adequate and appropriate in the circumstances for rendering first-aid to his employees if they are injured or become ill at work; and for this purpose a person shall not be suitable unless he has undergone -

(a) such training and has such qualifications as the Health and Safety Executive may approve for the time being in respect of that case or class of case, and

(b) such additional training, if any, as may be appropriate in the circumstances of that case.

3(2)

ACOP

Suitable persons

1   A 'suitable person' is:

(a) a first-aider who holds a current first-aid certificate issued by an organisation whose training and qualifications were, at the time of the issue of the certificate, approved by the Health and Safety Executive for the purposes of the regulations. In certain circumstances a first-aider will need additional or specific training to be a 'suitable person';

(b) any other person who has undergone training and obtained qualifications approved by the Health and Safety Executive for the purposes of the regulations.

3(2)

Guidance

2   Practising registered medical practitioners, and practising nurses whose names are entered on Part 1, 2 or 7 of the Single Professional Register maintained by the United Kingdom Central Council for Nursing, Midwifery and Health Visiting may be regarded as first-aiders for the purpose of the Approved Code of Practice.

3(2)

ACOP

Criteria for deciding adequate and appropriate provision of first-aiders

3   It is impossible to lay down any precise ratio of first-aiders to employees which can be adopted in all cases. All relevant factors need to be taken into account. These include the distribution of employees within the establishment, the nature of the work, the size and location of the establishment, whether there is shift working, and the distance from outside medical services, as well as the number of employees. The number of first-aiders provided by the employer should be determined on the basis of all the relevant factors and not solely on the numbers of employees at work.

4   Where an undertaking presents specific or unusual hazards, then at least one of the suitable persons should have received additional or specialised training particular to the first-aid requirements of the employer's undertaking.

5   First-aiders should be accessible to the majority of the workforce, or situated where an injury is most likely to occur. However, such centralised arrangements might not be suitable for a large plant with fewer employees dispersed over a wide area. In such conditions the principles set out in 3(1) paragraph 10 should be followed.

3(2)

ACOP

Provision of first-aiders when access to treatment is difficult

6 When access to places of treatment outside the establishment is difficult, eg because the place of work is a long distance from accident and emergency facilities, there is likely to be a need for one or more first-aiders to be provided irrespective of the nature of the undertaking or the numbers of employees.

Provision of first-aiders when employees of more than one employer are working together

7 When employees of more than one employer are working together and the employers concerned wish to avoid duplication of provision, they should make an agreement whereby one of them provides the necessary first-aid personnel. Where such an agreement is made, the general principles set out in 3(1) paragraph 6 should be followed.

Provision of first-aiders when employees work away from employer's premises

8 In the case of employees who regularly work away from their employer's establishment in isolated locations or where the work involves travelling long distances in remote areas from which access to accident and emergency facilities may be difficult, consideration should be given to training in emergency first aid (see 3(2) paragraphs 28 and 29). Where, in addition, potentially dangerous tools or machinery are used, it may be necessary for one or more members of the group to be first-aiders.

Numbers of employees and appointed persons

9 In any undertaking the more employees there are, the greater is the probability of injury or illness occurring at work. The number of employees should not be regarded as the only factor in deciding whether first-aiders are needed and, if they are, how many would be appropriate. The employer has to provide, as a minimum, an **appointed person** at all times when employees are at work. In low risk situations, eg offices or libraries, an employer will need one first-aider during normal working hours for every 50 employees. In hazardous situations the employer should decide what numbers of first-aiders will be adequate and appropriate, but this should not be less than one for every 50 employees. Where there is shift-working, the employer should ensure that adequate and appropriate first-aid provision is available for each shift. An employer may provide any number of first-aiders in addition to the requirements of this Approved Code of Practice even in situations where a first-aider is not identified as being essential.

Guidance

Recruitment and selection of first-aiders

10 In order to ensure that there is an adequate number of first-aiders in the establishment, an employer may, from time to time, need to recruit or select personnel, suitable to undergo first-aid training. The employer should bear in mind the requirements of the course and the qualities likely to make a good first-aider. It is essential that people who are reliable and likely to remain calm in an emergency are selected. In addition, a first-aider should have the aptitude and ability to cope with an intense course of study and be able to use the knowledge and skills learnt during the course. The duties can be physically demanding and first-aiders should be free of any condition which would affect their capability.

11 In selecting first-aiders, it is important that the other tasks on which the first-aider is employed should be such as to allow him or her to leave them immediately and go rapidly to the scene of an emergency.

12 A written record of the dates on which first-aiders obtained their certificates, including certificates in additional or specific hazard first-aid training, and refresher training should be kept.

13 Employers who experience difficulty in recruiting suitable persons to enable them to fulfil their first-aid obligations should seek advice from the local Employment Nursing Adviser. A list of offices where Employment Nursing Advisers are located is given in Appendix 1.

Appropriate training for first-aiders

14 In most instances, training and qualifications in general first aid approved by HSE (3(2) paragraph 20) will suffice. However, in cases where there is

(a) a danger of poisoning by certain cyanides and related compounds

(b) a danger of burns from hydrofluoric acid, and

(c) a need for oxygen as an adjunct to resuscitation

first-aiders will need to undergo specific training (see 3(2) paragraphs 24 to 27) approved by HSE, in addition to general first-aid training.

15 In certain other cases (eg where there is a serious risk of gassing, or of exposure to toxic chemicals etc) the first-aider may need to undergo *'such additional training as may be appropriate in the circumstances of the case'*.

16 When planning to introduce any new process, the employer should consider whether additional or specific hazard training for first-aiders will be necessary. If there is a need for first-aiders to undergo further training and an employer has difficulty in arranging for such training to be given, advice can be obtained from the local Employment Nursing Adviser (see Appendix 1).

Access to skilled advice

17 In many cases, the first-aider's skills will be used while the help of medical or nursing personnel, or the ambulance service, is obtained. First aid as defined in regulation 2 also includes treatment of minor injuries which will not always need the services of medical or nursing personnel. The first-aider may on occasion need medical or nursing advice on general matters associated with this minor aspect of first aid. Employers should ensure, therefore, that first-aiders are aware of possible sources of such advice, for example, from workplaces with occupational health services, organisations whose training and qualifications are approved by HSE, or through the local office of HSE's Employment Medical Advisory Service.

Recording first-aid treatment

18 Records of all cases treated should be made and kept in a suitable place, eg alongside first-aid equipment. They should always be readily available. (A suggested form of record-keeping is given in Appendix 2.)

Approval of first-aid training and qualifications

19 Any organisation, or individual employer, may seek approval to train and examine first-aiders and award certificates of qualification in first aid.

20 The criteria to which HSE will have regard in deciding whether to approve the training and qualifications given include:

(a) that the qualifications and training of trainers conform with guidance issued by HSE (see 3(2) paragraphs 30 and 31);

(b) that the proposed syllabus includes both theoretical and practical work and conforms with guidance issued by HSE (see 3(2) paragraph 22);

(c) that equipment listed in 3(1) paragraph 16 is used for training and examination purposes;

(d) that suitable arrangements are made for conducting examinations which should be carried out by independent examiners as specified in 3(2) paragraph 32 and who have not been involved in the training of the candidates they examine;

(e) that training organisations only accept for first aid at work courses individuals whose intention it is to practise first aid in the workplace during the validity of the first-aid certificate; and

(f) that suitable premises are available for training and examination purposes.

21 Courses will be monitored by HSE staff and in cases where standards of training are not maintained steps will be taken to revoke the approval issued to the training organisation. Training courses, including examinations, should be of at least four full days' duration (six contact hours per day) or the equivalent, allowing the course to run over a longer period. Each session should be of not less than two hours' duration and the whole course (including examination) must be completed within 13 weeks from the date of its commencement. Due to monitoring requirements courses cannot be held outside the UK.

22 The following subjects should be included in the syllabus:

(a) resuscitation;

(b) treatment and control of bleeding;

(c) treatment of shock;

(d) management of the unconscious casualty;

(e) contents of first-aid boxes and their use;

(f) purchasing first-aid supplies;

(g) transport of casualties;

(h) recognition of illness;

(i) treatment of injuries to bones, muscles and joints;

(j) treatment of minor injuries;

(k) treatment of burns and scalds;

(l) eye irrigation;

(m) poisons;

(n) simple record keeping;

Guidance

(o) personal hygiene in treating wounds: reference to Hepatitis B and Human Immunodeficiency Virus with regard to first-aiders; and

(p) communication and delegation in an emergency.

Refresher courses

23 Certificates of Qualification in first aid will be valid for such a period of time as HSE directs (at present for three years). A refresher course, followed by examination, will be required before recertification. Refresher courses should be of at least two days' (six contact hours per day) duration including time set aside for examination. Each session should be of not less than two hours' duration and the whole course (including examination) must be completed within six weeks from the date of its commencement. Courses should include revision of all subjects included in the basic syllabus together with theoretical and practical training in any new first-aid methods and procedures. Where a certificate has lapsed, it will be necessary for the person to complete a full first-aid course.

First-aid training where specific hazards exist

24 In cases where there is

(a) a danger of poisoning by certain cyanides or related compounds

(b) a danger of burns from hydrofluoric acid, or

(c) a need for oxygen as an adjunct to resuscitation

training should be carried out by organisations approved by HSE for training in these specific hazards. Organisations wishing to participate in such training should seek approval from HSE. Approval to carry out specific training may be given to suitable organisations which are not otherwise approved for first-aid training. Organisations should submit their proposed syllabus and details of trainers and examiners to HSE for approval.

25 Such training should include the following items:

(a) the nature of the hazard and methods of preventing its effects;

(b) symptoms, signs and treatment of conditions produced by adverse effects of the hazard;

(c) pharmacological action of antidotes, if any, and risks associated with administration of antidotes to unaffected casualties;

(d) practical training in the checking and use of appropriate equipment; and

(e) maintenance of detailed records of incidents where additional methods of first-aid treatment are used.

26 The duration of courses will vary depending on the subject matter. The minimum duration of a course in a particular subject will be determined by HSE. The training should be given by suitable persons as defined in 3(2) paragraph 30 or by a person who has special knowledge of and expertise in the use of the particular first-aid technique required.

27 Following successful completion of a course, which should include an examination carried out by a suitable independent person (3(2) paragraph 32),

a candidate will be awarded a certificate. Certificates will be valid for such period of time as HSE directs and refresher courses, followed by re-examination, will be required before recertification.

Emergency first-aid training

28   Training in emergency first aid may be given at the workplace by occupational health staff or in short courses run by organisations whose training and qualifications for first-aiders are approved by HSE. Emergency first-aid training should be considered for appointed persons and employees working in small groups away from their employer's establishment or where a specific hazard exists.

29   Short courses of at least four contact hours' duration should include the following items:

(a)   resuscitation;

(b)   control of bleeding;

(c)   treatment of the unconscious casualty; and

(d)   communication, contents of first-aid box and, where appropriate, treatment of the effects of specific hazards existing at the workplace.

This training should be repeated as a minimum, every three years.

First-aid trainers and examiners

30   All trainers and examiners should either have been active in first aid in the workplace, or been employed in an Occupational Health Service and should be competent to teach. Organisations wishing to train lay trainers for this purpose should seek the approval of HSE.

First-aid training should be given by:

(a)   registered medical practitioners, or nurses whose names are entered on Part 1, 2 or 7 of the single professional register maintained by the United Kingdom Central Council for Nursing, Midwifery and Health Visiting, with knowledge and experience of first aid in the workplace; or

(b)   qualified teachers/graduate lecturers who hold a current first-aid certificate from organisations whose training and qualifications for first-aiders are approved by HSE, and who have practical experience of first aid in the workplace; or

(c)   lay trainers who hold a certificate which is issued by an organisation whose training of lay first-aid trainers is acceptable to HSE and which shows they have a high level of theoretical and practical knowledge of first aid in the workplace, and that they are competent to teach. The certificate must be renewed every three years.

31   Any trainer who is to participate for the first time in a first aid at work course or examination after 2 July 1990 will need to satisfy the criteria set out above (3(1) paragraph 30). First-aid trainers whose names were accepted by HSE before 2 July 1990 may continue to instruct and examine on first aid at work courses. Lay trainers whose certificates are due for renewal will need to attend a full four day course in instructional techniques (3(2) paragraph 38).

Guidance

32   First-aid examinations should be conducted by at least two examiners who are qualified trainers, one of whom should be a nurse or medical practitioner with knowledge and experience of first aid in the workplace.

First-aid examinations

33   The examination should cover both theory and practice. Every candidate should be required to demonstrate proficiency in resuscitation, control of bleeding and treatment of the unconscious patient.

34   Examiners should not have participated in the training of any of the group to be examined. Candidates should be afforded the same privacy as in any other formal examination. For this reason candidates may not act as casualties during the examination and must be examined on an individual basis. If necessary, lecturers and trainers can act as casualties.

35   Two separate rooms, one for practical examinations and one for theoretical examinations, should be provided. A waiting room should be made available to hold candidates either before or after examinations.

Training for first-aid lay trainers

36   Candidates for training as lay trainers should hold a current certificate or qualification in first aid issued by an organisation following a course of training approved by HSE and should have held such a certificate for at least three years.

37   Lay trainers whose certificates are due for renewal will need to attend a full four day course in instructional techniques.

38 Training courses established to prepare lay trainers for the certificate referred to in 3(2) paragraph 30c should satisfy the following criteria:

(a)   the minimum duration of training courses should be four days (six contact hours per day) or the equivalent, including time taken for final assessment;

(b)   training should be carried out by lecturers/tutors who are experienced in teaching methods and have knowledge and experience of first aid in the workplace;

(c)   one lecturer/tutor should be identified as the person responsible for all course arrangements;

(d)   the syllabus of training should include the rationale behind the application of first-aid treatments, instruction and practice in teaching methods and the use of audio-visual aids as well as teaching of practical demonstration methods and practical training in answering questions posed by class members; and

(e)   final assessment of each candidate's suitability to hold a lay trainer's certificate should be carried out by two independent assessors, one of whom should be either a qualified occupational health nurse or a registered medical practitioner with knowledge and experience of first aid in the workplace.

39   Reassessment of lay trainers should be carried out every three years by approved, independent assessors, following an update of teaching methods and current first-aid practice. During assessment, the students should demonstrate the ability to provide competent training.

Regulation

(3) Where a person provided under paragraph (2) is absent in temporary and exceptional circumstances it shall be sufficient compliance with that paragraph if the employer appoints a person, or ensures that a person is appointed, to take charge of -

(a) the situation relating to an injured or ill employee who will need help from a medical practitioner or nurse, and

(b) the equipment and facilities provided under paragraph (1)

throughout the period of any such absence.

(4) Where having regard to -

(a) the nature of the undertaking, and

(b) the number of employees at work, and

(c) the location of the establishment,

it would be adequate and appropriate if instead of a person for rendering first-aid there was a person appointed to take charge as in paragraph (3)(a) and (b), then instead of complying with paragraph (2) the employer may appoint such a person, or ensure that such a person is appointed.

3(3)-3(4)

ACOP

1   An appointed person is a person provided by the employer to take charge of the situation (eg to call an ambulance) if a serious injury/illness occurs in the absence of a first-aider. The appointed person can render emergency first aid if trained to do so. Ideally all appointed persons should receive training in emergency first aid (3(2) paragraphs 28-29). An appointed person is also responsible for first-aid equipment in the absence of a first-aider.

2   In exceptional circumstances during the temporary absence of the first-aider, an employer is required to provide an appointed person. Employers should note that appointed persons are not, except in the case stated below, an acceptable full-time alternative to a first-aider and it is therefore essential that, other than in exceptional circumstances, there are sufficient numbers of first-aiders to provide coverage at all times when employees are at work. **Foreseeable absences, such as planned annual leave, are not considered to be 'exceptional and temporary circumstances' in this respect**. The only exception to the above is in the case of establishments where, because of the nature and location of the undertaking, there are no specific hazards and the number of employees is small.

3(3)-3(4)

Regulation 4

Duty of employer to inform his employees of the arrangements made in connection with first-aid

Regulation 4

An employer shall inform his employees of the arrangements that have been made in connection with the provision of first-aid, including the location of equipment, facilities and personnel.

ACOP 4

1   The employer should ensure that all employees are told of the location of first-aid equipment, personnel and facilities when they first join the establishment. This should always be part of any induction training given to new employees at the time of their joining the establishment. If employees

ACOP

subsequently move to another part of the establishment, they should be told where first-aid personnel, equipment and facilities are located, if different from their previous place of work.

2   There should be at least one notice posted in a conspicuous position in all workplaces within the establishment, including central offices from which peripatetic employees work, giving the locations of first-aid equipment and facilities and the name(s) and location(s) of the personnel concerned.

3   The notices should be in English, and a version in any language commonly used at the establishment may be displayed alongside the English version. The actual location of equipment should be clearly identified. Where the Safety Signs Regulations 1980* apply, the identification should comply with them.

*S.I. 1980/1471.

Regulation 5

Duty of self-employed person to provide first-aid equipment

A self-employed person shall provide, or ensure that there is provided, such equipment, if any, as is adequate and appropriate in the circumstances to enable him to render first-aid to himself while he is at work.

ACOP

1   Self-employed persons whose work involves few hazards, eg accountants, typists, management consultants, should provide themselves with first-aid equipment adequate and suitable to their needs, for example, a small travelling first-aid kit might be sufficient. Self-employed persons whose occupations involve hazards such as the use of potentially dangerous tools or machinery, should provide themselves with suitable first-aid equipment depending on the nature of the hazard.

2   Where a self-employed person is working on premises under the control of an employer or with other self-employed persons, it is the responsibility of each self-employed person to provide or ensure that there is provided such first-aid equipment as is adequate and appropriate for themselves. However, if the persons concerned wish to avoid duplication of provision they may make an agreement that one of them provides the necessary equipment. In that case the other still has to ensure that adequate and appropriate provision is made. Where such an agreement is made, the general principles set out in 3(1) paragraph 6 for agreement between employers should be followed.

Regulation 6

Power to grant exemptions

(1)   Subject to paragraph (2), the Health and Safety Executive may, by a certificate in writing, exempt any person or class of persons, from any of the requirements imposed by these Regulations, and any such exemption may be granted subject to conditions and to a limit of time and may be revoked at any time.

(2)   The Executive shall not grant any such exemption unless, having regard to the circumstances of the case, and in particular to -

(a)   the conditions, if any, which it proposes to attach to the exemption, and

(b) any other requirements imposed by or under any enactment which apply to the case,

it is satisfied that the health, safety and welfare of employees and self-employed persons and the health and safety of other persons who are likely to be affected by the exemption will not be prejudiced in consequence of it.

Cases where these Regulations do not apply

These Regulations shall not apply -

(a) where the Diving Operations at Work Regulations 1981[a] apply;

(b) where the Merchant Shipping (Medical Scales) (Fishing Vessels) Regulations 1974[b] apply;

(c) where the Merchant Shipping (Medical Scales) Regulations 1974[c] apply;

(d) on vessels which are registered outside the United Kingdom;

(e) to a mine of coal, stratified ironstone, shale or fireclay;

(f) in respect of the armed forces of the Crown and any force to which any provision of the Visiting Forces Act 1952[d] applies.

(a) S.I. 1981/399.
(b) S.I. 1974/1192.
(c) S.I. 1974/1193.
(d) 1952 c. 67.

Application to miscellaneous mines

In their application to mines not excluded from these Regulations by Regulation 7(e), Regulations 3 and 4 shall have effect as if the manager for the time being of any such mine were an employer and as if the persons employed were his employees.

Application offshore

Subject to Regulation 7, these Regulations shall apply to and in relation to any premises or activity to or in relation to which sections 1 to 59 of the Health and Safety at Work etc. Act 1974 apply by virtue of Articles 6 and 7(a), (b) and (d) of the Health and Safety at Work etc. Act 1974 (Application outside Great Britain) Order 1977[e] (which relate respectively to mines extending beyond Great Britain and to certain activities concerning vessels and construction works in territorial waters).

(e) S.I. 1977/1232.

Repeals, revocations and modification

(1) The enactments mentioned in column (1) of Schedule 1 are hereby repealed to the extent specified opposite thereto in column (3) of that Schedule.

(2) The Orders and Regulations mentioned in column (1) of Schedule 2 are hereby revoked to the extent specified opposite thereto in column (3) of that Schedule.

(3) Section 91(1) of the Mines and Quarries Act 1954 shall be modified by after the words "every mine" inserting the words "of coal, stratified ironstone, shale or fireclay".

Schedule 1

Repeals
Regulation 10(1)

(1) Short title	(2) Chapter	(3) Extent of repeal
The Mines and Quarries Act 1954.	1954 c. 70; relevant amending instrument is SI 1974/2013.	In section 115, the words "section ninety-one (save in so far as it relates to persons employed below ground)" and in paragraph (a) the words "and ninety-one".
The Agriculture (Safety, Health and Welfare Provisions) Act 1956.	1956 c. 49.	Section 6(1) and (4).
The Factories Act 1961.	1961 c. 34.	Section 61.
The Offices, Shops and Railway Premises Act 1963.	1963 c. 41.	Section 24.

Schedule 2

Revocations
Regulation 10(2)

(1) Regulations or Order	(2) Reference	(3) Extent of revocation
The Wool, Goat-Hair and Camel-Hair Regulations 1905.	SR & O 1905/1293.	Regulation 15.
The Horsehair Regulations 1907.	SR & O 1907/984.	Regulation 9(d).
The Ambulance and First-Aid Arrangements at Blast Furnaces, Copper Mills, Iron Mills, Foundries and Metal Works Order 1917.	SR & O 1917/1067; amended by SR & O 1925/863 and SI 1961/2434.	The whole Order.
The Saw Mills and Wood-working Factories Welfare (Ambulance and First Aid) Order 1918.	SR & O 1918/1489; amended by SR & O 1925/864 and SI 1961/2434.	The whole Order.
The Hides and Skins Regulations 1921.	SR & O 1921/2076.	Regulation 1.
The Chemical Works Regulations 1922.	SR & O 1922/731; relevant amending instruments are SI 1961/2435, 1981/16.	Regulations 10(a), 12, 13, 14 and 17(2)(g).

Schedule 2

(1) Regulations or Order	(2) Reference	(3) Extent of revocation
Order dated 24th August 1925 revoking provisions in the Ambulance and First-Aid Arrangements at Blast Furnaces, Copper Mills, Iron Mills, Foundries and Metal Works Order 1917.	SR & O 1925/863.	The whole Order.
Order dated 24th August 1925 revoking provisions in the Saw Mills and Woodworking Factories Welfare (Ambulance and First Aid) Order 1918.	SR & O 1925/864.	The whole Order.
The Herring Curing (Scotland) Welfare Order 1926.	SR & O 1926/535; to which there are amendments not relevant to these Regulations.	Articles 3 and 4.
The Herring Curing Welfare Order 1927.	SR & O 1927/813, amended by SI 1960/1690.	Articles 3 and 4.
The Oil Cake Welfare Order 1929.	SR & O 1929/534.	Article 7.
The Docks Regulations 1934.	SR & O 1934/279, to which there are amendments not relevant to these Regulations.	Regulations 4 to 8.
The Clay Works (Welfare) Special Regulations 1948.	SI 1948/1547.	Regulation 7 and the Schedule.
The Miscellaneous Mines (General) Regulations 1956.	SI 1956/1778.	Regulation 71.
The Quarries (General) Regulations 1956.	SI 1956/1780.	Regulation 38.
The Agriculture (First Aid) Regulations 1957.	SI 1957/940.	The whole Regulations.
The First-aid Boxes in Factories Order 1959.	SI 1959/906; relevant amending instrument is SI 1961/1250.	The whole Order.
The Docks (First-aid Boxes) Order 1959.	SI 1959/2081.	The whole Order.
The First-aid (Standard of Training) Order 1960.	SI 1960/1612; relevant amending instrument is SI 1961/1250.	The whole Order.
The First-aid (Revocation) Regulations 1960.	SI 1960/1690.	The whole Regulations.
The First-aid Boxes (Miscellaneous Industries) Order 1960.	SI 1960/1691.	The whole Order.
The Shipbuilding and Ship-repairing Regulations 1960.	SI 1960/1932, to which there are amendments not relevant to these Regulations.	Regulation 79 and Schedule 3.

(1)	(2)	(3)
Regulations or Order	Reference	Extent of revocation
The Railway Running Sheds Order 1961.	SI 1961/1250.	Paragraphs 8 and 9 of the Schedule.
The Blast Furnaces and Saw Mills Ambulance (Amendment) Regulations 1961.	SI 1961/2434.	The whole Regulations.
The Chemical Works Ambulance (Amendment) Regulations 1961.	SI 1961/2435.	The whole Regulations.
The Docks (Training in First-aid) Regulations 1962.	SI 1962/241.	The whole Regulations.
The Offices, Shops and Railway Premises First Aid Order 1964.	SI 1964/970; relevant amending instrument is SI 1974/1943.	The whole Order.
The Offices and Shops in Factories (First Aid) Regulations 1964.	SI 1964/1321.	The whole Regulations.
The Offices at Building Operations &c. (First Aid) Regulations 1964.	SI 1964/1322.	The whole Regulations.
The Offices in Electrical Stations (First Aid) Regulations 1964.	SI 1964/1323.	The whole Regulations.
The Information for Employees Regulations 1965.	SI 1965/307.	Paragraph 26 of the Schedule.
The Construction (Health and Welfare) Regulations 1966.	SI 1966/95, amended by SI 1974/209.	In Regulation 3(2), the words from "'certificate in first-aid' does not" to "or over" and from "'training organisation'" to "of these Regulations". In Regulation 4(2), the figures "5, 8, 9". Regulations 5 to 10. The Schedule.
The Ionising Radiations (Unsealed Radioactive Substances) Regulations 1968.	SI 1968/780; to which there are amendments not relevant to these Regulations.	Regulation 44(2).
The Abstract of Factories Act Order 1973.	SI 1973/7.	Paragraph 39 of Schedule 1.
The Factories Act General Register Order 1973.	SI 1973/8.	Part 7 of Schedule 1 and Part 5 of Schedule 2.
The Construction (Health and Welfare) (Amendment) Regulations 1974.	SI 1974/209.	The whole Regulations.
The Offices, Shops and Railway Premises Act 1963 (Repeals and Modifications) Regulations 1974.	SI 1974/1943.	Regulation 3(2).
The Chemical Works (Metrication) Regulations 1981.	SI 1981/16.	All entries in the Schedule relating to Regulation 12 of the Chemical Works Regulations 1922.

Appendix 1 — Addresses of Employment Nursing Advisers

Tyne and Wear, Northumberland	Arden House Regent Centre Regent Farm Road Gosforth NE3 3JN Telephone 091-284 8448
North Yorkshire and West Yorkshire	8 St Pauls Street Leeds Yorkshire LS1 2LE Telephone 0532-446191
Nottinghamshire, Derbyshire	Birbeck House Trinity Square Nottingham NG1 4AU Telephone 0602-470712
South Yorkshire and Humberside	Sovereign House 40 Silver Street Sheffield S1 2ES Telephone 0742-739081
Norfolk	Kiln House Pottergate Norwich NR2 1DA Telephone 0603-615711
Bedfordshire, Buckinghamshire, Cambridgeshire, Hertfordshire	14 Cardiff Road Luton Beds LU1 1PP Telephone 0582-34121
London Boroughs of Bexley, Croydon, Greenwich, Hillingdon, Hounslow, Hayes, Kingston-upon-Thames, Lambeth, Lewisham, Merton, Richmond upon Thames, Southwark, Sutton, Wandsworth, South London, Waterloo	1 Long Lane Southwark London SE1 4PG Telephone 071-407 8911
London Boroughs of Middlesex, Barnet, Brent, Camden, Ealing, Enfield, Hammersmith, Fulham, Harrow, Kensington, Chelsea, Westminster and City, Wembley, Uxbridge, Southall, Romford, Dagenham, Ilford, Hornchurch, Upminster	Chancel House Neasden Lane London NW10 2UD Telephone 081-459 8855
Avon, Gloucestershire, Somerset	Inter City House (2nd floor) Mitchell Lane Victoria Street Bristol BS1 6AN Telephone 0272-290681

Devon, Cornwall	6th Floor Phoenix House Notte Street Plymouth PL1 2RB Telephone 0752-668481
East Midlands, Northamptonshire, Leicestershire, Warwickshire, Oxfordshire	Belgrave House 1 Greyfriars Northampton NN1 2BS Telephone 0604 21233
Kent, Surrey, East Sussex, West Sussex	3 East Grinstead House London Road East Grinstead West Sussex R19 1RR Telephone 0342-326922
Hampshire, Wiltshire, Berkshire, Dorset, Isle of Wight	Priestley House Priestley Street Basingstoke RG24 9NM Telephone 0256-473181
Suffolk, Essex	39 Baddow Road Chelmsford Essex CM2 0HL Telephone 0245-284661
London Boroughs of Barking, Hackney, Haringey, Havering, Islington, Newham, Redbridge, Tower Hamlets, Waltham Forest, Footscray, Bethnal Green, East Smithfield	Maritime House 1 Linton Road Barking Essex IG11 8HF Telephone 081-594 5522
North Wales	Crown Buildings 31 Chester Street Wrexham Clwyd Telephone 0978-290500
South Wales	Brunel House (13th floor) 2 Fitzalan Road Cardiff CF2 1SH Telephone 0222-473777
Birmingham, West Midlands, Wolves, Walsall	McLaren Building 2 Masshouse Circus Queensway Birmingham B4 7NP Telephone 021-200 2299
Staffordshire and Salop, Hereford and Worcester (County)	The Marches House Midway Newcastle-under-Lyme Staffs ST5 1DT Telephone 0782-717181

Greater Manchester	Quay House Quay Street Manchester M3 3JE Telephone 061-831 7111
Merseyside, Cheshire	The Triad 19th Floor Stanley Road Bootle Merseyside L20 3PG Telephone 051-922 7211
Cumbria and Lancashire	Victoria House Ormskirk Road Preston Lancs PR1 1HH Telephone 0772-59321
Scotland: Borders, Lothian, East and North Scotland	Belford House 59 Belford Road Edinburgh EH4 3UE Telephone 031-225 1313
Scotland: Central, West and South Scotland	314 St Vincent Street Glasgow G3 8XG Telephone 041-204 2646
Aberdeen, Highlands, Caithness, Sutherland, Orkney and Shetland, Invernessshire	Greyfriars House Gallowgate Aberdeen AB9 2ZU Telephone 0224-649549

Format for recording first-aid treatment

Full name & address of persons who suffered an accident	Occupation	Date when entry made	Date and time of accident	Place & circumstances of accident - (state clearly the work process being performed at the time of the accident)	Details of injury suffered and treatment given	Signature of person making this entry (state address if different from column 1)
(1)	(2)	(3)	(4)	(5)	(6)	(7)

Annexe

General first-aid guidance for inclusion in first-aid boxes

Note

This guidance is intended for inclusion in first-aid boxes (or similar containers) in the form of a stout card or leaflet (see 3(1) paragraph 16a).

The Crown waives its right to copyright in respect of the text and illustrations contained in this Annexe. Thus the Annexe may be reproduced by eg suppliers of first-aid boxes and included in these boxes. Any person reproducing the Annexe should inform

> The Chief Employment Nursing Adviser, Health and Safety Executive, Health Policy Division, Daniel House, Trinity Road, Bootle L20 7HE

so that they can be notified of any future revisions of the guidance.

HSE wishes to express its thanks to the Resuscitation Council for allowing the use of their illustrations shown on pages 27 and 28.

Health and Safety (First-Aid) Regulations 1981

General guidance for first aid at work

NOTE: TAKE CARE NOT TO BECOME A CASUALTY YOURSELF WHILE ADMINISTERING FIRST AID. USE PROTECTIVE CLOTHING AND EQUIPMENT WHERE NECESSARY.

TREATMENT POSITION

Casualties should be seated or lying down when being treated, as appropriate.

Advice on treatment

If you need help send for it immediately. If an ambulance is needed, arrangements should be made for it to be directed to the scene without delay.

Priorities in first aid

(1) **BREATHING**

IF CASUALTY IS NOT BREATHING

Place in a horizontal position, face upwards.

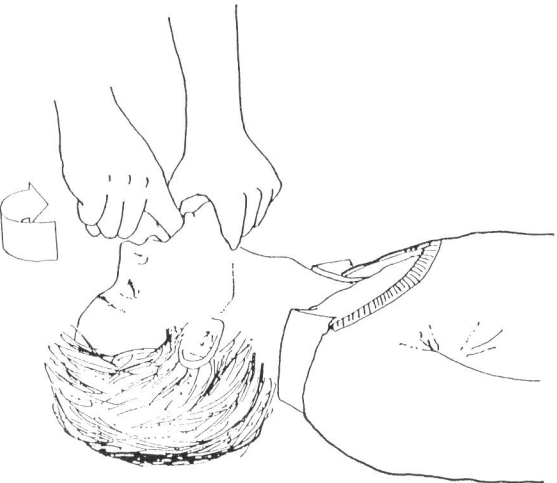

Open and clear mouth.

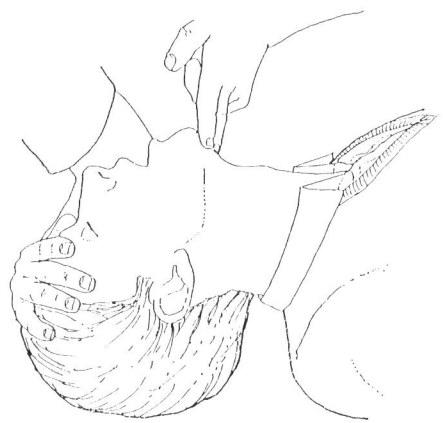

Lift chin forward while pressing forehead back with other hand. Maintain this position throughout.

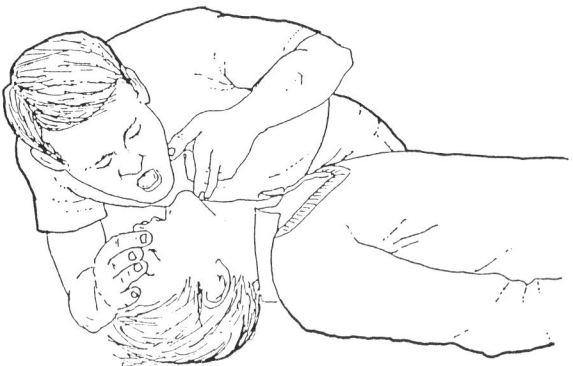

Kneel beside casualty. While keeping his head tilted backwards, open his mouth and pinch his nose.

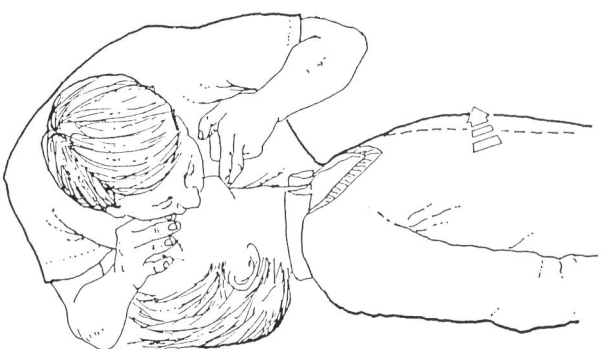

Open your mouth, take a deep breath. Seal his mouth with yours and breathe out firmly into it. Casualty's chest should rise.

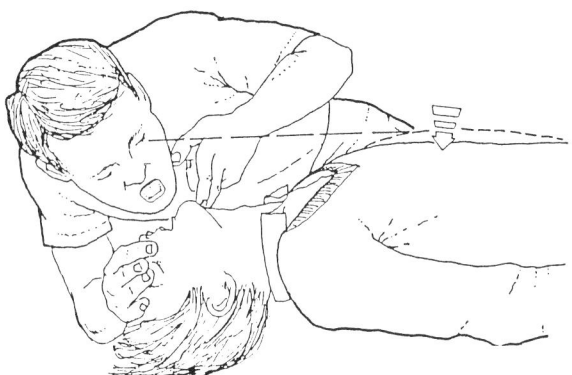

Then remove your mouth and let his chest fall. If chest does not rise, check head is tilted back sufficiently. Continue at a rate of 12 - 16 times a minute until the casualty is breathing by himself.

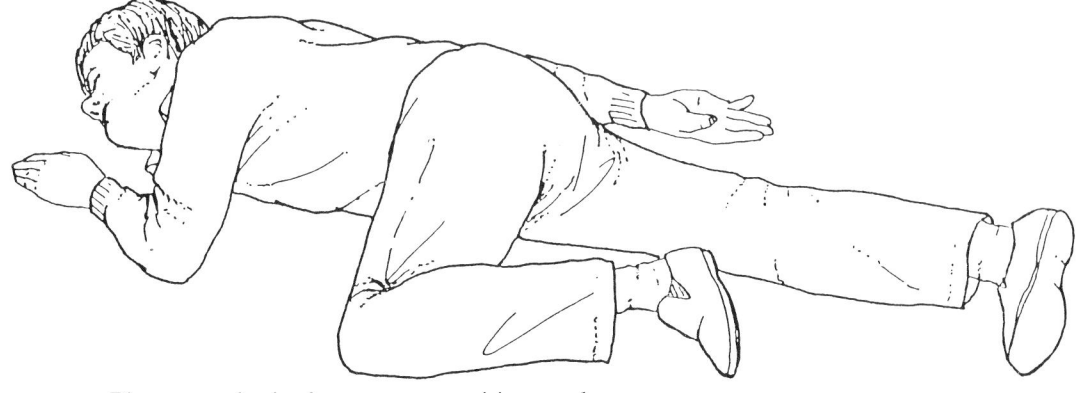

Place casualty in the recovery position as shown.

(2) **UNCONSCIOUSNESS**

Keep the airway open by clearing the mouth and making sure the tongue does not block the back of the throat.

Put casualty in the recovery position.

(3) **BLEEDING**

Wash your hands if possible.

Control by direct pressure (using fingers and thumb) on the bleeding point. Apply a dressing.

Raising the bleeding limb (unless it is broken) will help reduce the flow of blood.

(4) **SUSPECTED BROKEN BONES**

Do not move the casualty unless he is in a position which exposes him to immediate danger.

Support the injured parts and secure them so they cannot move.

(5) **BURNS**

(i) **BURNS AND SCALDS**

Wash your hands if possible.

Do not remove clothing sticking to the burns or scalds or burst blisters.

If burns and scalds are small, flush with plenty of clean, cool water before applying a sterilised dressing.

If burns are large or deep, wash your hands, apply a dry sterile dressing and send to hospital.

(ii) **CHEMICAL BURNS**

Avoid contaminating yourself with the chemical.

Remove any contaminated clothing which is not stuck to the skin.

Flush with plenty of clean, cool water for 10-15 minutes.

Apply a sterilised dressing to exposed, damaged skin and send to hospital.

(6) **EYES**

Wash your hands if possible.

Foreign bodies in the eye: Irrigate eye to remove loose material with clean cool water.

Chemical in the eye: Flush the open eye continuously with clean, cool water for 10-15 minutes.

People with eye injuries should be sent to hospital, the eye covered with an eye pad.

(7) ELECTRIC SHOCK

Do not touch the casualty until the current is switched off.

If the current cannot be switched off, stand on some dry insulating material and use a wooden or plastic implement to free the casualty from the electrical source.

If breathing has stopped, start mouth to mouth resuscitation and continue until casualty starts to breathe by himself or until professional help arrives.

(8) GASSING

Use suitable protective equipment.

Move casualty to fresh air.

If breathing has stopped, start mouth to mouth resuscitation, continue until casualty starts to breathe by himself or until professional help arrives.

Send to hospital with a note of the gas involved.

(9) MINOR INJURIES

Casualties with minor injuries of a sort they would attend to themselves if at home may wash their hands and apply a small sterilised dressing from the first-aid box.

(10) RECORD KEEPING

An entry of each case dealt with must be made in the accident book.

(11) FIRST-AID MATERIALS

Each article used from the first-aid box should be replaced as soon as possible.